Avoiding The Leadership Trap

12 Traits That Will Derail Your Career

&

Diminish Your Leadership Impact

Avoiding the Leadership Trap: 12 Traits that Will Derail Your Career & Diminish Your Leadership Impact

©2018. Cherita Weatherspoon

ISBN 978-0-9983130-7-8 (ebook)

ISBN 978-0-9983130-6-1 (paperback)

Published by Spoonfed Motivation Publications

To order copies of this book, email:

Dr. Cherita Weatherspoon at

info@alcstrategy.com

Disclaimer:
This book is for informational purposes only. The author/ publisher makes no claims or guarantees of outcomes or success. The content in this book should not be considered as counseling or other professional advice. Readers may implement the information included at their discretion.

*Many thanks to Regan, Joanne, Joan, Mike,
Frank and Tara.
Your leadership fuels the work that I do.*

Table of Contents

Introduction ix

Why Leaders Are Important.. xiii

Good Leaders vs. Bad Leaders xvii

What Happens When Leaders Fail xix

Trap 1   A Lack Of Vision 1

Trap 2   Failing To Communicate 3

Trap 3   Always The Know It All.. 7

Trap 4   Failing To Listen 9

Trap 5   Conflict Avoidance 11

Trap 6   Abdicating Responsibility 13

Trap 7   Failing To Learn From Mistakes......................... 15

Trap 8   Overzealous Or Reluctant To Change 17

Trap 9   A Lack Of Humility 19

Trap 10   A Lack Of Empathy 21

Trap 11   A Lack Of Emotional Intelligence 23

Trap 12   A Lack Of Integrity...................................... 27

What To Do When You Fail As A Leader 31

Conclusion 35

Mission Critical Consulting Leadership Training & Coaching 37

Introduction

There are people who desire leadership,
and there are those who avoid it.

Some people want to be in leadership because they desire to impact change, to help people, or to make a difference in some way. Others desire leadership because it is a way to have power, control, and notoriety. While these latter three things aren't innately bad, when in the hands of the wrong leader they can be destructive.

Sometimes people who start off in leadership roles with good intentions fall into the leadership trap. They become influenced by the influence they wield; they get power hungry or drunk off the control that they have over other people. Other leaders come to find it easier to make decisions based on how the outcome impacts them personally rather than on the impact it has on the organization. Still, others find it difficult to choose the ethical route when easier and more profitable options are in front of them. Falling into the leadership trap can happen to anyone, even to you, especially when you don't realize you're falling.

❧

There is a lot to learn from bad leaders, perhaps even more than what you may learn from great leaders. It's easy to look at some of our greatest leaders and learn lessons on inspiring and motivating others. We can identify traits and habits that can help us be more effective in our leadership, like boldness and surrounding ourselves with people who have skill sets that complement our skills. The thing to keep in mind, however, is that a bad leader is bad behind closed doors long before they are bad in public view and what you see in the public view isn't always representative of the real person.

In fact, the most valuable lessons in leadership may not come from leaders themselves but from those that they lead - the people who sit face to face and eye to eye with them; who see them when goals are being achieved and when failure comes unexpectedly; who are on the receiving end of their disappointments and frustrations; and who see them under pressure. Our teams, our follower groups, even people in our families and social circles are the best judge of our leadership - not what the media says about us, not even what our leaders say about us, and certainly not what we say about ourselves.

Yes, you may know how to get things done. You may know how to make money. These *things*, however, don't make you a great leader. How you *do* these things is what determines how great a leader you are.

❧

In *Avoiding the Leadership Trap*, you will learn why leaders are important, the differences between good leaders and bad leaders, what happens when leaders fail, what to do when you fail as a leader, and the twelve traits to avoid if you want to be a great leader.

My goal with this book is to help you identify areas of growth for yourself – whether you are currently in a leadership position (regardless of the level) or you aspire to become a leader.

Leadership is a fluid process and you will, at least you should, constantly develop your leadership skill. You don't become a good leader and remain a good leader, just as you don't become a bad leader and are doomed to stay that way. What works for one organization may not work for another. What works for one team in an organization may not work for a different team in the same organization. Therefore, how you navigate the leadership traps identified here may vary from team to team and organization to organization, but the traps are real and will follow you wherever your leadership takes you.

Why Leaders
Are Important

*Every vision needs a champion, and every
mission requires someone to lead the charge.*

Most great ideas, historical movements, and dramatic cultural transformations started at the grassroots level – people who cared and who were willing to do the work. But without leadership most, if not all, these advancements would not have occurred. You see, every vision needs a champion and every mission requires someone to lead the charge. However, in most cases, it's impossible to do it alone. When people come together on a mission, it's important to have someone focused on steering everyone in the right direction and other people to help manage, motivate, and move smaller groups towards specific goals that will contribute to the mission's success. These are leaders. Their roles are extremely important. Without leaders, people will be left to interpret directives in their own way, to make decisions about resources, to determine what the priorities are, to do whatever they think is best for the organization, or to choose to do nothing. This would inevitably lead to chaos.

Leaders help to **communicate a common goal** and **harness the power of their human, financial, time and**

other resources in contributing to the achievement of that goal. Without leadership, many dreams, witty inventions, innovations, and ideas for technological advances would never come to fruition.

Leaders help **solve problems**. Not being limited by their own experience and knowledge, a true leader will be resourceful in figuring out a solution to a problem. They know how to tap into the genius and creativity of their team and how to collaborate with others.

Leaders help to **keep the Visionary informed** about what is happening in the organization. Leaders are in tune with the pulse of the organization and are aware of cultural shifts that may impact vision fulfillment.

Leaders help to **evaluate goal progression** and **identify how to do things better**. They are forward-looking while being able to determine where and how things are in the present, remaining aware of lessons learned from the past, and simultaneously adapting to stay on track to the goal.

Leaders **champion the Champion**. They support the senior most leader in casting and communicating the vision and leading their teams in doing the work necessary to accomplish the vision. They stand by corporate decisions and help to gain buy-in. They work diligently to build systems and a culture that reflects the vision, mission, and goals of the Champion.

Leaders **champion the team**. They support their people and advocate for their needs. They defend the team when they are wrongly attacked or blamed. They work to ensure that they have the resources to perform their jobs well. They hold the team accountable while taking responsibility for coaching, directing, disciplining, managing, mentoring and leading. They work to develop their team members, not only in team roles but in their careers and as future leaders.

Leaders **steward the organization's most valuable asset**, its people. They help their people to feel connected to the organization and valued by the organization. Leaders ensure their people know how their work impacts the mission. They provide clarity around organizational goals and changes, and they demonstrate to their people that business is not just about business, but it's also about people -the people in the organization and the people the organization serves.

The importance of leadership cannot be understated.

Good Leaders vs. Bad Leaders

*People make daily decisions in their leadership roles
that will distinguish them as a good leader or a bad leader.*

Some people believe the idea that people are born leaders. I disagree; however, I do believe that people are born with character traits that make them more likely to be good leaders. I also believe that people can learn to be good leaders and they can develop the traits that others may have been born with. Ultimately, I believe that people make daily decisions in their leadership roles that will distinguish them as a good leader or a bad leader.

I want to make the distinction between effective leadership and good leadership. You can be an effective leader – cast a vision, gain support, motivate people to act, and accomplish your goal – and perhaps you can do it while stepping into every trap described in this book. But that alone does not make you a good leader. Hitler, as an obvious example, was an effective leader, but certainly not a good one.

Conversely, you can be a good leader and perhaps not as effective as one would desire, and still find yourself making your way up the leadership ladder because many organizations value people skills over hard skills. If you have excellent people skills, know how to build a team with complementary skill sets and expertise, and can avoid these twelve leadership traps, you can be both a good leader and an effective leader.

One distinguishing trait of a good leader is recognizing that there is always room to grow. A good leader has humility and is not overly confident or arrogant. They recognize the difference between edification for influence and self-aggrandizing. They never stop learning and regardless of their position, they never come to the conclusion that they've fully arrived. A good leader will surround themselves with people who will challenge them and help make them better. They will have other leaders who they admire and mentors who help keep them on course for both personal and professional success.

What Happens When Leaders Fail

Your success does not come without the impact of people, and your failures do not occur without impacting people.

There are multiple ways in which a leader can fail. They can fail to meet a deadline, to accomplish a goal, to communicate effectively, to lead, to manage, to assess, or to plan, among others. Perhaps what is more important than the ways a leader can fail is the impact of their failure.

When a leader fails, it tends to have a ripple effect, either upwards, downwards or cross-organizationally, and sometimes the failure is so far-reaching that its effect will spread in each direction. Of course, there is the obvious impact of the failure. For example, if the VP of Sales didn't hit the sales target, the failure to generate that revenue is going to have an impact on future goals, profit margins, and perhaps on that VPs job. However, its impact is likely more far-reaching than that. That loss of revenue may impact the jobs of people on the sales team (and, if not their jobs, their bonuses). It may impact the jobs of support staff, the organization's ability to fund planned research and development, employee lifestyles and personal lives as expectations to perform and meet new goals increase, or the board's evaluation of the CEO. It may even impact stock price and shareholder dividends.

I recognize that not every leadership failure will have such dramatic effects on so many areas, but more failures than not will have some impact on things and people in addition to and, in some cases, other than the leader who failed.

Noting this here is important to remind you that when you are in leadership, it is never just about you. Your success does not come without the impact of people, and your failures do not occur without impacting people.

TRAP 1

A Lack Of Vision

There should be a consistent overarching vision that influences your decisions and keeps your team focused and motivated.

A leader without a clear picture of where they are going is not a leader; they are a wanderer. Your team needs direction, but not random or vague generalizations about where you are going, why you are going and what to do to get there. You must be able to point them in a definitive direction and provide guideposts along the way.

Understandably, if you are in a new leadership role, it will take some time to get clear on where you are now, what your resources are, and the best path to take to get to where it is you determine you are going. However, you should have garnered enough information through your interview process and initial meetings with your leaders and team to have developed a general idea about where you are leading people and why.

When in a new role it is ideal to have a plan to gather the information and do the assessments necessary to gain a solid understanding of your area of responsibility and the culture of the organization in which it operates. Being able to communicate your plan and acting on it will help you acquire the patience and support you need from your team until the vision is clearly developed.

If you have been in your role for some time and haven't communicated a vision to your team or leadership, it's not too late to do so. Review your organization's mission and get clear on your role in it. Talk to your people. Find out what's working and what's not. Determine what they need to do their best work. Talk to your leadership. What are their goals for your area? What changes do they want to see? Then plan, implement, evaluate, revise and repeat – making sure to communicate with your team along the way.

Escape Strategy

The circumstances that exist at the time you set and declare your vision will not always exist. Resources change, priorities shift, and people come and go. As a result, you can expect to have to make some changes in your plan along the way. However, your vision does not have to (and should not) change every time the strategy or your tactics change. There should be a consistent overarching vision that influences your decisions and keeps your team focused and motivated. Stay resolute in the vision, but remain flexible in your plan to getting there.

TRAP 2

Failing To Communicate

Communication is not always easy, but it is always necessary.

Communication is a major key to leadership success. The words "Does not communicate" or "Does not communicate well" are often included in lists of poor leadership qualities and are often found in the performance evaluations of people who desire a leadership role but cannot seem to find an opportunity.

Communication is a broad concept and, to be fair, it's not always clear what is meant when someone uses the phrase "communicate well." As a leader, assume that it means everything that it can possibly mean: tone of voice, volume of voice, articulation, vocabulary, public speaking, written communication, body language, facial expressions, etc. That is not to say that you must be excellent in each of these areas, but it would be wise to recognize that people are judging you on all these areas. Perhaps the most important component of communication, however, is the ability to express your thoughts clearly and in a way that can be received by the parties with whom you are communicating. This requires adaptability. The way you communicate at executive board meetings may be different than how you communicate with your team. How you communicate in a large group of people may be different from your communication in a more intimate setting. You also need to be able to communicate effectively with stakeholders at all levels of the organization, with different personality types, and during times of crises.

Having the ability to communicate well means nothing if you don't do it. Leaders sometimes avoid communicating because they want to avoid conflict and questions. Sometimes leaders avoid communicating because they want to be in control. Both traits will cause you problems in the workplace. Your communication with your team is just as important as your communication with your peers and your leaders. If you don't communicate with your team, they will come up with their own ideas and scenarios about what is going on in the organization, which is likely to impact commitment and productivity. You cannot effectively lead if you cannot or do not effectively communicate.

Escape Strategy

Communication is not always easy, but it is always necessary. When you fail to communicate, you fail to provide leadership, stability, and security, even in times of instability and insecurity. A lack of communication -whether up, down or across - will lead to people developing their own ideas about what is going on, which most likely will not be in your favor. Be willing to have the difficult conversations, to ease tensions, inform, console, direct, acknowledge, and appreciate. While you may have a communication fail, the biggest communication failure is not to communicate. If you are unsure about how, when or what to communicate in a sensitive situation, find a trusted mentor, colleague or friend (at the same professional level or higher) who you can bounce your ideas off or even practice with. This will help you feel more confident in your communication and help you minimize communication failures.

TRAP 3

Always The Know It All

Thinking you know it all will prevent you from acknowledging your own weaknesses and building a team that can address those weaknesses.

One of the easiest traps for a leader to fall in is thinking they know it all. It's as if holding a leadership position somehow transforms them into the organization's resident genius. No matter what the question is, they have the answer. Regardless of problem, they have the solution. Despite the situation, their idea is always the best idea.

This one trap alone can stop you from progressing any further than where you are as a leader. You see, a great leader will never act like they know it all because they recognize that no one can possibly know it all and that there are always different perspectives to be considered. The tendency to think you know it all usually follows a pattern. Because you think you know it all, you don't seek advice or other opinions; then you don't admit when you are wrong, and you may choose to give bad answers, advice or solutions rather than admit that you don't know.

Thinking you know it all will prevent you from acknowledging your own weaknesses and building a team that can address those weaknesses. It will also have you step boldly into situations that are over your head and, in the long run, hold you back from accomplishing your goals. Thinking you know it all can also alienate the people who are on your team – whether above or below you, causing them to avoid you and perhaps even watch you flounder and flail when you've gotten yourself into a situation that you can't handle.

Escape Strategy

While it may be true that your answers, solutions, and ideas got you into your leadership position, the fact is that it was another leader who recognized that they didn't know it all that provided you the opportunity to share your thoughts, act on them, and prove that you had more to offer the organization. Be that same kind of leader, one who recognizes that she/he doesn't have to have all the answers, just the resourcefulness to get the answers.

TRAP 4

Failing To Listen

Listening is an act of respect.

This trap is akin to "Always the Know It All," but it focuses on how receptive you are to the ideas and perspectives of others. You can be so confident in yourself that you won't listen to the counsel of others or consider ideas from your team.

Listening does not mean that you must take action on everything that is presented to you, but it does mean that you recognize that there may be some benefit in what others have to say. Listening is acknowledging that you don't have all the information or knowledge that exists on any particular topic and that your experience is not the sum of all valuable experience that can influence a situation.

Being open to hear what others have to say and learning from the experience of others will benefit you in the long run. People higher than you will be open to mentoring or coaching you, your peers will be willing to share opportunities with you, and those you lead will be comfortable sharing ideas with you that could help fuel your success.

Escape Strategy

Listening is an act of respect. When you listen to the people on your team, they will feel valued. When they feel valued, they will be more committed to their work and to your success. Also, remember that the act of listening is inclusive of your body language and response to what you are hearing. Make sure that your body language, attitude and verbal response is respectful so that the other parties feel heard. Don't listen to be able to say that you listened. Listen to hear what others are really saying.

TRAP 5

Conflict Avoidance

Conflict comes with leadership, and it can't
be avoided if you want to be successful.

Most people do not enjoy conflict, and many try to avoid it. While it's natural to want everything to go smoothly, have everyone like you, and not have to address difficult issues; a leader doesn't have the luxury of sitting idly by, hoping this is the case, and avoiding uneasy situations. Sometimes you are going to have to initiate hard conversations, address problems with team members, and call people on the carpet for their behavior. Sometimes, you're going to be on the receiving end, having to listen to harsh words and negative opinions. Conflict comes with leadership, and it can't be avoided if you want to be successful.

If you avoid addressing issues because you are afraid of conflict, you will not only look weak; you will set yourself up for failure. It will be difficult to advocate for yourself or for your team if you try to avoid conflict. It will be hard to get buy-in for new ideas if you aren't willing to have difficult conversations. It will be virtually impossible to manage your team if you can't direct them, coach them, or even discipline them because it makes you uncomfortable.

Conflict is unavoidable and trying to avoid it is likely just going to cause more conflict. While there is no need to go into every meeting ready for a fight or even to assume that every conversation must be based on an assumption of conflict, when conflict does arise, you need to be ready to address it and lead through it.

Escape Strategy

Conflict is a natural part of life, and it is not necessarily a bad thing. A lot of good can come from conflict – creative ideas, innovative solutions, new alliances, greater understanding, and better positioning, among other things. Try to view conflict as both an opportunity to learn and to grow, not only for the other parties involved but for you as well. Entering conflict with this perspective will help you better manage whatever the situation may be.

TRAP 6

Abdicating Responsibility

You can't be responsible for the successes produced under your leadership and not simultaneously be responsible for the failures.

Responsibility is a core part of leadership. Abdicating responsibility when things don't go right or when times are rough will make you untrustworthy, not only to those who work for you but to those who you work for. As the leader, you are responsible for getting results. You are responsible for the success or failure of your team. If you or your team are not producing or in some other way failing to meet goals, it falls on you.

You must be intentional about avoiding this trap because it's very easy to take credit when things are going well and then keep quiet when they are not. However, you can't be responsible for the successes produced under your leadership and not simultaneously be responsible for the failures produced under your leadership. I've witnessed leaders use the word "I" much too often when sharing accomplishments for their area of responsibility and then choose to use the words "you" and "they" when things don't go as planned. This type of behavior will erode morale and cause you to lose the support and respect of your team very quickly. Conversely, taking responsibility can help build your team's support of you and foster greater commitment to you and your success.

Sometimes, as the leader, you will have to take the fall, the blame, and the whispers that come with missing the mark. That is what you signed up for.

Escape Strategy

The reality is that while you are responsible, you may not always be the one to be held accountable. Even in those times, take the opportunity to be reflective about what you could have done differently. Could you have made better decisions? Where could you have intervened? Who should you have assigned? Identify your role in the situation – because you did have a role – so you can do better the next time.

TRAP 7

Failing To Learn From Mistakes

No one expects you not to make mistakes. They expect you, as a leader, to own up to them, correct them, and learn from them.

You are bound to make mistakes. Every leader does. The key is to learn from the mistake. Leaders who fail to learn from their mistakes are: 1) sure to repeat them and 2) foolish.

A mistake is simply an opportunity to learn. While some of these "opportunities" will be painful and perhaps even humiliating, there is still something to be learned. However, to learn the lesson, you must first be willing to admit and acknowledge the mistake. This relates to Traps 3 (Always the Know It All) and 6 (Abdicating Responsibility). Recognize when you've made a mistake, repair what you can, then analyze the situation. Identify what you could have done differently. Assess the information or data that you used to make your decisions. Determine the best path forward. Be honest about what happened and share what you learned with those who were impacted by your mistake. Apologize when appropriate. Follow this process with your team, teaching them to do the same when they make a mistake. This will help you to avoid making the same mistake again while building confidence for future decisions and opportunities.

Failing to learn from your mistakes is a foolish thing to do. It assumes that your mistake had no impact, it demonstrates a lack of leadership, a denial of responsibility, and it communicates a lack of concern for your organization. All these things can damage your professional reputation and put you in jeopardy of losing the respect of your team and maybe your position.

Escape Strategy

Being a leader does not exempt you from making mistakes. It does, however, make the cost of your mistakes higher, more impactful, and perhaps more critical to the organization. For these reasons, it is imperative that you learn from your mistakes. The higher you move in leadership, the more dangerous your mistakes can be for your organization and neither you or the company can afford to have you repeating the same mistakes or failing to apply lessons learned from one mistake to a different situation. No one expects you not to make mistakes. They expect you, as a leader, to own up to them, correct them (to the extent possible), and learn from them. In a later chapter, I share the proprietary process I developed and use in my own life to learn from the mistakes I make. You may find it helpful for you.

TRAP 8

Overzealous Or Reluctant To Change

Most leaders understand that change is difficult, but the fact that it is does not justify a refusal to change.

We are living in a time where change not only comes, it comes quickly, and it comes often. Trying to keep up with all the change to remain relevant and competitive can be exhausting and a losing strategy. Yet, some leaders choose this method of operation. They want to respond to every new trend, try the latest technology, and constantly update their methodology – even though they haven't given anything a real chance to work. These leaders believe that the next greatest thing is the best thing for their organization. This is not necessarily true. As a leader, you must be able to evaluate what's working and identify what you need to do to address the things that are not. It's typically not an entire overhaul of a system or a completely new organizational structure – at least not every year. In trying to leave a mark and make an impact, leaders can be overzealous in embracing change. This can put your department or organization in a constant change of flux, leaving it unstable and your people feeling insecure, which will have a negative effect on employee morale and productivity, and likely profits and other success outcomes.

On the other side of the spectrum, you have leaders who are reluctant to embrace change. These leaders are afraid of what change might mean for them and their team. They are comfortable with how things are because it is familiar and predictable. Embracing change may mean a new way of thinking, being, and doing for them. It also may mean that they are no longer the expert and may perhaps be less valuable to an organization as a result of a change. Reluctancy to change, however, may be worse than the change itself. If an organization has decided to move forward, refusing to move with them may leave you standing on the sidelines watching the organization progress without you. Most leaders understand that change is difficult, but the fact that it is does not justify a refusal to change.

Escape Strategy

There will be times when you are leading change and times when change is forced upon you. You will have to decide if the direction the organization is heading is in alignment with your values, the mission, and vision of the organization and if you are committed to giving your best to the organization despite the change.

Your leadership in the face of change will be important to guiding your team through the change with as little difficulty as possible. Avoiding all the traps described in this book can help you navigate the change process. The worst thing you can do, however, is to make the change process more difficult because of your attitude and your conversation.

TRAP 9

A Lack Of Humility

You have never really arrived. You are simply
where you are at this point in time.

Reaching a certain level in your career or attaining a long-desired position can be exhilarating. It's likely that you'll feel that your hard work finally paid off and that you deserved the role. While that's likely true, and you have every right to be excited, proud, and confident in what you'll do in the role, you want to be careful that your confidence doesn't turn into cockiness.

Leadership or more specifically power, influence and notoriety (even if it's only within an organization) can change people. It's as if ascending to a level of leadership or a certain level of responsibility, or attaining a certain title, or even earning a certain salary somehow sets them apart from everyone who has not. It's a feeling of having "arrived." Even in this role, no matter how great it is, there is still further to go; if not another position, certainly in personal and professional growth. It's important to remember that you have never really arrived. You are simply where you are at this point in time.

Leaders who lack humility are often polarizing. Either you love them, or you hate them. You respect them, or you don't. The challenge with this is that, as a leader, one of your responsibilities is to unite and bring people together in support of a common goal. You may be thinking as you read this, "I don't care if people love me or respect me," but don't get stuck there; it's more serious than that. I've found that when people think you have a huge ego, that you think you are better than everyone else, or that you are cocky, they will root for your downfall. They may even participate in it. Because of your high and arrogant attitude, they want to see you brought low. If you are in leadership, the last thing you want to have is your team, your peers, or your leaders wanting you to fail and perhaps setting you up to fail.

People tend to be attracted to confidence, while they avoid cockiness. Be confident, but be humble. Don't forget your journey to success. Don't dismiss others because they are not where you are. Don't allow your position, prestige or paycheck to interfere with your ability or willingness to connect with people, to listen to people, and to help people.

Escape Strategy

A lack of humility is often demonstrated through words. Be careful of how you talk to people and mindful of the words that come out of your mouth. Don't talk down to people, but seek opportunities to build people up. Don't talk about people, advocate for people instead. Don't be so focused on celebrating your own successes. Find opportunities to celebrate the success of others. Remember that it's not about you; it's about the team, and each member of the team is valuable. Be sure they know that.

TRAP 10

A Lack Of Empathy

Your position does not exclude you from
recognizing the humanity of the people you lead.

There are leaders who seem to be "in tune" with their people. They are understanding and compassionate, even in difficult situations. Then there are leaders who are inclined to believe that because their people are "below" them, they are somehow less deserving of understanding and compassion. In challenging times, this mindset gets stronger, and the resulting behaviors make a bad situation worse. The ability to show empathy will help move a leader far in their career. Knowing how to put yourself in other people's shoes will help you to earn the respect of your team. They will follow you, support you, and even fight for you when your leaders are coming down on you because they know you value them.

Showing empathy does not mean that you refrain from setting standards, dealing with inappropriate behaviors or performance issues. Nor does it mean that you avoid making tough decisions that need to be made for the organization's benefit. It simply means that you understand

and acknowledge the impact of those things on your people and do your best to minimize the blow rather than being uncaring and singularly focused on the business decision. The demonstration of empathy is not an indication of weakness. In fact, it is a sign of strength. It is much easier to keep emotional distance from a situation and to forget about the people who are impacted by it. When you don't care, it's easier to sleep at night. But it takes courage to look people in the eye, give them the space to express themselves, hear them, understand them, and to show compassion even when you can't change the outcome.

Escape Strategy

There are always people impacted by your decisions and your behavior. Your position does not exclude you from recognizing the humanity of the people you lead. Nor do the positions your people hold make them any less deserving of being treated with dignity and respect. Believe in the value of empathy and demonstrate it with the people you lead. There will likely come a time in your career when you'll need it from your team.

TRAP 11

A Lack Of Emotional Intelligence

Emotional Intelligence can help you build strong relationships; a lack of it can destroy relationships.

Emotional Intelligence (EI) is the ability to recognize your emotions and those of others, distinguish and label different feelings, and use this awareness to inform your thinking and behavior in adapting to various environments or in supporting your goals. Simply stated, emotional intelligence is the ability to manage emotions, both your own and those of others. It is different from empathy in that empathy is about feeling what others are feeling – putting yourself in their shoes. Both are important.

A lack of emotional intelligence will prevent you from being able to empathize. It will also minimize your awareness of your own emotions and how you may be handling them, whether it be internally or how they are being demonstrated to the world. This can lead to increased stress and inappropriate displays of anger and frustration. You'll also have problems tuning into the emotional state of your team members and others around you, which can lead to inappropriate emotional reactions on both sides, a breakdown in communication, and a decrease in morale. A decrease in morale will inevitably lead to a decrease in productivity. A decrease in productivity will negatively impact your organization's profits and/or other success outcomes.

Emotional intelligence can help you build strong relationships; a lack of it can destroy relationships. The good thing is that you can develop your emotional intelligence. Start by focusing on your own emotions – becoming more self-aware of what you are feeling, what those feelings mean, and what you are doing with those feelings. Ask yourself if what you are doing is helping you or hurting you. Then work on being intentional about understanding the emotions of those you work with. Try to identify the emotion, what it means for them, and how it might be guiding their behavior. Process this information and use this awareness to guide your behavior, your attitude, and your responses. Use your understanding of the emotional environment to communicate more effectively, to motivate, to calm, to reassure, and to direct. Remember that emotional intelligence is not just about awareness, but what you do with that awareness – how you adapt to the situation or environment to meet your goals.

Escape Strategy

Practice emotional intelligence regularly. Be committed to developing your EI for both your benefit and that of the people you work with. Be present, be observant, ask "why" questions, listen to what is being said and listen for what is not being said. Allow space for others to feel and process their emotions without taking offense. Use your awareness to help guide them through the process. Be open to the experience and honest with yourself about what you are experiencing. Developing a high level of emotional intelligence is first an internal process before it is an external process.

TRAP 12

A Lack Of Integrity

When all is said and done, all you have is
your word and the behaviors that follow it.

If you are in a leadership role and do not have integrity, you are no leader. Perhaps you are a con artist, manipulator, liar or even a thief. But you are not a leader. When all is said and done, all you have is your word and the behaviors that follow it. What you say matters. What you do matters. You should have an established personal code of honor that guides how you lead your people.

I intentionally used the word *personal* as opposed to *professional* because I do not believe that a lapse in integrity in one part of your life is unique to that part of your life. If you lack integrity at work, it's almost guaranteed that you lack it outside of work as well.

I want to be clear that I am not talking about situations where you find yourself in a dilemma and are not clear on what the right decision is, and you end up making the wrong decision. I am talking about intentional, perhaps even planned, breaches of integrity.

How do you know if you lack integrity in your leadership? The breaches I described above may serve to protect or benefit you or the organization in some way, or they may be designed to hurt other people. You know the act is wrong, but you do it anyway. It can be as simple as lying or as complicated as framing someone for a crime. It may be an action of questionable ethics or something illegal. Wherever it falls on the spectrum, it is inappropriate and unbecoming of a leader.

As a leader, people are putting their trust in you – the people who hired you and the people you lead. Do not lie to them. Do not deceive them. Do not manipulate them. Most importantly, do not allow them to turn you into someone you are not. Stand by your word, and if something changes and prevents you from doing so, communicate that to those impacted by it. When you are being asked about confidential things, state that you're not at liberty to discuss or share, but that you will share if, and when, you can. Don't lie to avoid the conversation. Do what you say you are going to do. Be honest, even when it's difficult.

Your team and the leaders of your organization should know what to expect from you. When you lack integrity in how you operate and deal with people, people will not know what to expect from you and will, as a result, distrust you, try to avoid you, and even go behind your back or over your head to check to see if you are telling the truth, doing the right thing, or if they should follow your lead. There may be times when being out of integrity helps you move up the ladder. Don't fall for the trap! Eventually, this will backfire on you, and you'll find yourself on the receiving end of a lack of integrity wondering how you got in this position. Worse, you may find yourself on the front cover of the newspaper at the center of a scandal or in jail.

Choosing to lead with integrity may be an easy choice, but it will not always be easy to live out that choice. You will face difficult decisions. You will be privy to information that can cause hurt, harm or alarm. Furthermore, you will have authority that gives you a level of influence over the lives of other people. Sometimes you may be tempted to choose in your favor even when it's not the right or best thing to do. Sometimes you may want to punish people or take revenge for a real or perceived wrong. These thoughts are natural, but what separates good leaders from bad leaders in these times is what you choose to do with the power you have.

Escape Strategy

You have a choice in the type of leader you are going to be, choose to be one who is worthy of the trust instilled in the position. Choose to be one that is worthy of the honor of being called leader. It's never too late to make that choice.

Life and leadership are much simpler when you choose to act with integrity. Choose to lead with integrity.

Find a mentor who will hold you accountable for your behaviors and actions and who can help guide you in making decisions that reflect a commitment to operating with integrity.

What To Do When You Fail As A Leader

The R$^{7™}$ Process is built on the inherent value of people and a commitment to operate in integrity regardless of how difficult the situation you face.

You will fail without a doubt. Hopefully, your successes will be far greater than your failures. But when those failures come, what can you do? I want to share a process that I developed over my years of experience leading teams at work, in my community, and in my home.

I found it necessary to be intentional about how I responded to failures - whether perceived or real. Being naturally task-oriented, I was always focused on the goal. That trait, unfortunately, caused me to sometimes forget about or give less attention to the people involved in achieving the goal. It wasn't that I didn't care about people, but sometimes I failed to consider what others thought and to communicate in sufficient detail. Sometimes, I would choose to do things myself because it was easier. I had the fortune of having a colleague hold a mirror up to me and very gently but directly give me feedback on ways that I might be "putting people off." Instead of getting offended, I reflected on what she shared, the examples she gave, and accepted that even though the impact of my behavior was not intentional it was still real and I had to change. This is when leadership and leadership impact became important to me. Not only was I very aware of my interactions and behaviors after this, but I was also very sensitive to how other leaders behaved and the impact of that behavior on the people they led.

Through reflection of self and observation of others combined with a strong desire to "do right by my people," I developed the *R7 Leadership Growth Process*™ as a way to engage in continuous growth as a leader by responsibly managing leadership failure.

The R7 Leadership Growth Process™

Review

Evaluate and analyze the details of what went wrong. Think about your decisions, the people involved, the resources that were utilized, the time allotted, the communication process, the established goal, and expected outcomes. Reviewing the failure is taking an in-depth look at the plan, the strategies, and the tactics and identifying what went wrong.

Reflect

Thoughtfully consider your decisions, actions, behaviors and attitudes and how they may have contributed to the outcome. Identify what you could have done differently in leading and managing the situation. Reflection is taking an in-depth look at yourself and the role you played in the failure.

Responsibility

Take ownership of the failure and your part in it. This is not just an internal, self-reflective process. You likely need to make a statement of responsibility to either your team, your peers or your leaders.

Revise

Utilize the knowledge gained in both *Review* and *Reflect* to determine a path forward. Modify your goal, the outcomes, and/or the plan; and make the necessary adjustments to your decisions, behaviors, attitudes or other elements that you know contributed to the failure.

Respond

Provide a mediated response to the appropriate interested and affected parties about the failure. Avoid having your communication cause additional damage by blame-shifting, showing anger, lying, or negating the impact of the failure.

Reconcile

When amends need to be made, do so. Then focus on using your communication skills to help those involved or impacted by the failure to process what has occurred, refocus on the future, and forge ahead.

Reconnect

Repeatedly reconnect your people and their work to the organization's vision. Provide clarity, ongoing communication, compassion, and concern while staying forward-focused.

The $R7^{™}$ process is simple, although not easy. While this process, or any other, may not always yield your desired results (i.e., saving your job or saving the jobs of others), it is built on the inherent value of people and a commitment to operate in integrity regardless of how difficult the situation you face. I recommend that you review it, internalize it and implement it as part of your leadership toolkit.

Conclusion

People are at the crux of your leadership success.

Being in leadership is not for the faint of heart. There are a lot of expectations and demands, and the pressure to perform comes from multiple directions. You will be talked about, blamed, mistreated, sometimes lied on, and perhaps even in a situation that you might describe as abusive or hostile. Deciding to lead is not a decision that should be taken lightly, not only because leadership can be challenging, but because a lot of responsibility comes with leadership. You are not only responsible for things and for goals, you are responsible for people. People who likely spend the majority of their waking or productive hours under your leadership. People who are likely giving more to you than they give to their own families or personal priorities in the way of time, energy and effort. Your leadership can literally make their lives more fulfilling or more stressful. That is a lot of power to wield, which is why how you lead is so important.

The twelve leadership traps described in this book are behaviors, traits and character flaws that I've identified in leaders who would very easily be called bad leaders. You'll notice that the traps had very little to do with skillset, expertise, or experience, but everything to do with how leaders interact and engage with people.

People are at the crux of your leadership success. You cannot produce without your people. You cannot profit without your people. While you may have some success operating in a way that devalues, dismisses or demeans your people, it is not sustainable, and you will never experience the success you could have if you embrace your people as your organization's most valuable asset.

I challenge you to be more intentional in your leadership. Start with identifying which of these leadership traps you need to get out of. Then define, in writing, who you want to be as a leader. Identify specific behaviors you need to change or actions you must take to progress in becoming this leader. Pay close attention to the leaders around you. What can you learn from them? What mistakes are they making that you should avoid? What strengths do they have that you need to develop? Finally, find a leadership mentor or coach who can help you along your journey. No matter where you are now – the level of position or years of leadership experience – there is always room to grow.

Aligned Leadership & Culture Solutions

Align Your Culture. Elevate Your Leadership.
Maximize Your Profit.

Learn more about our services and workshops at
ALCStrategy.com

NOTES